W9-DHV-726

THE STORY OF THE EARTH
RIVER

LIONEL BENDER

FRANKLIN WATTS
London · New York · Toronto · Sydney

© 1988 Franklin Watts

First published in Great Britain by
Franklin Watts
12a Golden Square
London W1

First published in the USA by
Franklin Watts Inc.
387 Park Avenue South
New York. N.Y. 10016

First published in Australia by
Franklin Watts Australia
14 Mars Road
Lane Cove
NSW 2066

UK ISBN: 0 86313 705 9
US ISBN: 0 531 10554 7
Library of Congress Catalog Card
No: 87 51705

Printed in Belgium

Consultant Dougal Dixon

Designed by Ben White

Picture research by Jan Croot

Produced by Lionheart Books
10 Chelmsford Square
London NW10 3AR

Illustrations:
Peter Bull Art

Photographs
Barnaby's Picture Library 25
J. Allan Cash Ltd 9, 13, 15, 26
GeoScience Features 8, 24–25, 27
Hutchinson Library *cover*, 31
Rex Features/Sipa Press 23
Tropix 14
ZEFA 1, 6, 7, 10, 11, 17, 19, 21, 22, 25, 29

THE STORY OF THE EARTH
RIVER

LIONEL BENDER

CONTENTS

This book tells the story of a typical river. It explains how the river is formed and what happens as it flows across country. It also looks at the different landscapes formed by rivers. Some rivers are small and slow-flowing. Others are huge and produce strong currents, sweeping aside rocks and boulders in their way.

▽ The illustration shows the complete story of a river. The river starts as a small trickle of water high in the mountains. Water always tries to flow to the lowest level, so the river runs downhill. On its way, it washes away soil and wears down rock. It first forms a valley and then a flat flood area or plain. Finally, it empties into the sea.

A river forms from rainwater that collects on mountains and hills. If the water cannot trickle underground, it runs downhill. As it heads toward the lowland, it flows along as a stream. At the bottom of the hill it is joined by other streams and becomes a large river. Now it flows more slowly and winds across country to the sea.

▽We have divided the story of our river into ten stages. In the following pages of the book we look at each stage in turn. There are photographs of rivers in different parts of the world. Diagrams explain how a river creates valleys and horseshoe-shaped lakes and forms rapids. We also look at how rivers affect plants, wildlife and people.

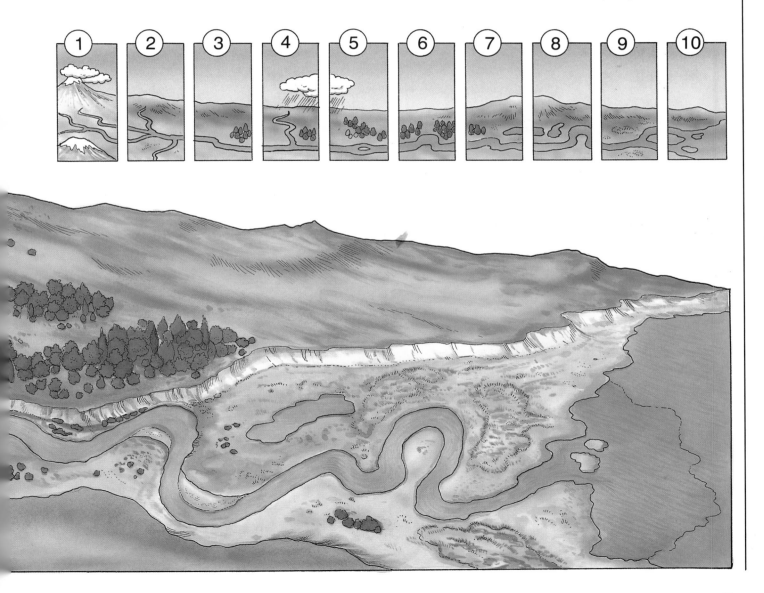

As winds blow across the oceans they pick up moisture. When the wind blows over mountains and hills, the moisture collects into tiny droplets of water and then into large drops. These fall to the ground as rain. The rainwater trickles through the surface and collects in tiny spaces between and within rocks on the mountainside.

Eventually, rocks overflow with water, which bubbles to the surface of the ground and flows downhill. The river is born. The start of a river is called a source and the trickle of water flowing from it is known as a spring.

▷Although rocks are solid, they contain many tiny spaces. These are usually filled with air but can fill with water instead. During heavy rains the spaces cannot take up all the water that falls on the rocks. Some of the water spills out and forms springs, like these in the Alps.

◁The source of a river can also be melting snow and ice. Here, on a mountaintop in Norway, snow has become packed down hard to form a mass of ice called a glacier. As the ice melts, water gushes out of the tip of the glacier and flows downhill as a tiny river or stream.

From the source high up on a mountain, water runs quickly down toward lower ground. The water washes away loose stones and earth, so the spring becomes gradually wider and deeper. Now as a small stream, the water starts to flow faster and more forcefully. It picks up loose pebbles and knocks away rocks on either side of the stream. These pebbles and rocks bounce and rattle along the bottom or bed of the stream. Eventually they carve out a groove or valley in the mountainside.

▽ Large chunks of rock have been washed along a stream bed in Switzerland to produce a rugged valley. Mountainous parts of the world such as Switzerland have many fast-flowing streams. The streams cut deep grooves and channels in the mountainsides.

△ In the Black Mountains in Wales, a stream has cut a winding, zigzag valley downhill.

◁Lower Falls in Yellowstone National Park in the United States. The Yellowstone River has worn away some of the rock to form a steep-sided valley called a gorge. Here, where the water flows over hard rock produced many millions of years ago by a volcano, the river drops down a cliff about 100 m (330 ft) high into a deep pool.

△The Iguazu River tumbles as a series of waterfalls over ledges of hard rock just before reaching the Paraná River in Brazil. A sequence of waterfalls, one after the other, is called a cascade. Thick clouds hang over the cascade. They are made up of fine droplets of spray thrown up by the river as it crashes down the falls.

The river reaches a cliff on the mountainside. The land drops away sharply and steeply. With nothing to stop it, the water tumbles over the cliff edge and falls straight down. The river becomes a waterfall.

The cliff has formed where the river meets a flat layer of hard rock. At the bottom of the cliff the rock is softer. The falling water gradually carves out a deep pool. In time the water will cut far back into the mountainside beneath the cliff edge. The cliff will collapse and a new waterfall will form further back along the river.

Up in the hills the river splashes and rolls over rocks. The water here flows fast and forms rough stretches called rapids.

Rapids are created where layers of hard rock beneath the river are sloping up or are tilted towards the surface. Soft rock sandwiched between the layers of hard rock is worn away more quickly by the river. The hard rocks start to stick out at the surface as ridges. Each time the water reaches a ridge, it is churned up.

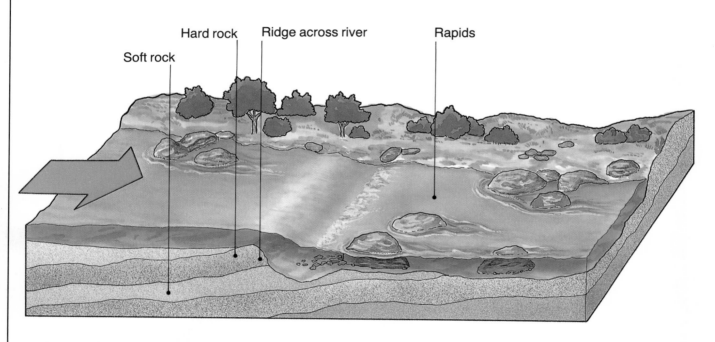

Soft rock   Hard rock   Ridge across river   Rapids

△ Rapids form where layers of hard rock stick up like ridges. Large rocks and boulders can also prevent the water from flowing smoothly. The quiet and gentle flow becomes a rough and noisy tumble of waves and swirling currents. The river now looks like a sea of foam.

▷ Rapids along a river in Norway. The river gets shallower here but flows more quickly than before, speeding up each time it tumbles over a ridge of hard rock. The water swirls in all directions. These movements of water within the river are called currents.

As the river flows down from the hills on to flatter ground, it loses much of its energy. The speed of the currents slows down and the water no longer splashes, bubbles and tumbles about as before. The river becomes calmer. It still carries along stones and sand grains but most of the rocky material falls to the bed of the river valley and stays there. Up in the hills the river bed was smooth rock. Here it is made up of loose sand and gravel.

▽ Instead of flowing down a steep slope as a single ribbon of water, a river sometimes spreads out and runs down in a fan-shape. Sand and stones carried along by the currents are dropped at the bottom of the slope. They form a mound of gravel, like this one in Death Valley, California.

△ This river, in the Yorkshire Dales, a hilly region of northern England, is flowing over the flat bottom of a valley. It weaves from side to side between the gentle slopes of the Dales. However, the currents are still swift and strong.

All kinds of plants and animals live in and around the river. Up in the mountains, conifer trees grow along the valley. On the lowland, broadleaf trees grow near the water's edge. In the water itself live weeds, tiny insects and snails. These are eaten by little fish and other animals such as water shrews. The little fish are eaten by bigger fish, which in turn are eaten by birds such as herons. Swallows fly over the water, feeding on dragonflies and other insects.

◁On the lowland, the river flows gently. Fish and other animals that live in the water do not have to be strong swimmers to avoid being swept away by the currents. Plants grow in the shallows along the river banks. As the river flows closer to the sea, it provides a home for more and more wildlife.

▽Among the water-loving reeds along the sides or banks of a river, a heron looks for a fish to eat. The bird's long legs allow it to stand in the water and to watch for passing fish.

The river has flowed down from the mountains on to the lowland. Now the currents are too weak to force a way ahead in a straight line. The river simply winds its way across the countryside in large curves or bends. As the water flows around each bend, it wears away more rocky material on the outside bank than on the inside bank. Sand and gravel removed from the outer bank drop to the river bed along the inner bank. In this way, over thousands of years, the river changes position. It gradually makes the valley wider.

▷ The inside bank of this river bend in France shows how the mass of sand has been built up gradually by the currents. Eventually the sandbank will be covered by plants. By that time the river will have cut away more of the outside of the bend and will have shifted its position.

▽ Just as a racing driver must take his or her car faster around the outside of a track to keep up with a car on the inside, so river currents are faster on the outside of each bend. On the inside bank the slower-moving currents drop sand and gravel carried by the river. Sandbanks are built up a little at a time.

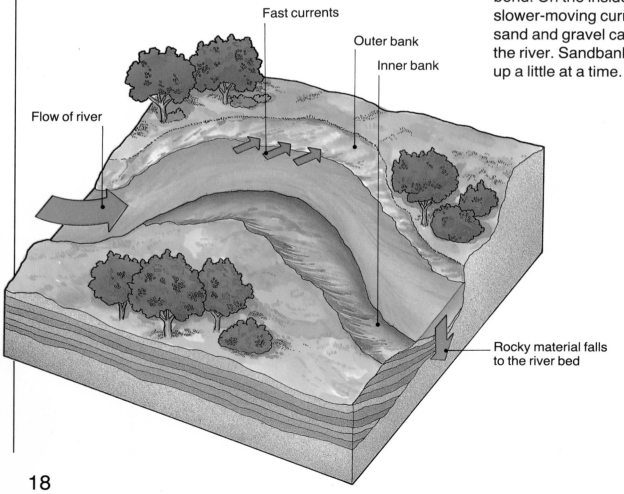

Fast currents

Outer bank

Inner bank

Flow of river

Rocky material falls to the river bed

The river now flows along lazily and silently. It weaves from side to side between bumps and mounds in the ground. In places it still curves gently, but it also forms tight bends or loops. It is as if the river is wandering around trying to find the easiest route to the sea.

The river currents no longer have enough energy to carry along stones and sand. The water does not flow in a valley but on a wide plain that has been built up from all the sand dropped by the river along its bed and banks.

▷ There may be so much sand and gravel dropped on the river bed that the river becomes raised up above the level of the plain. It then flows along a long thin platform or ridge. On this river plain, in Lapland, the river flows along a ridge. The old river banks mark the place where the river used to flow.

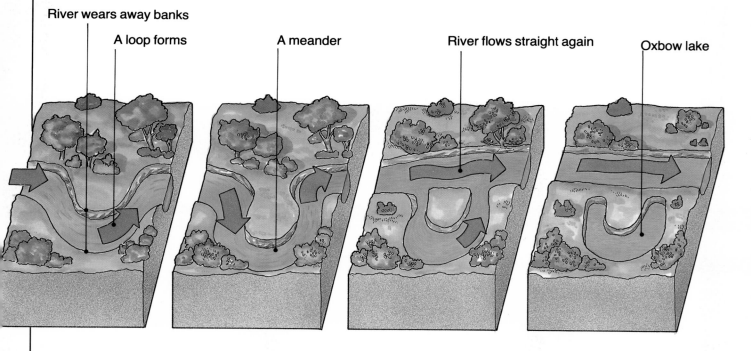

River wears away banks

A loop forms

A meander

River flows straight again

Oxbow lake

△ A river flowing over very flat land moves slowly in lazy curves or loops called meanders. As a river wears away the outside of each loop and builds up the inside, the meander becomes more U-shaped.

Eventually the river wears through the land within the meander and becomes straight again. The meander is cut off from the river and forms a horseshoe-shaped lake. This is called an oxbow.

After heavy rain or when mountain snow melts, the river becomes very full. Where the river zig-zags and flows gently along, the banks may not be high enough or strong enough to hold back the water. The river bursts its banks and floods. Murky water pours over the countryside. This is the river's flood plain. In times of flood, river water is full of sand and tiny pieces of soil, or silt. As this is washed on to the plain, it forms a rich, fertile soil. Flood plains make good farmland.

◁On its way to the sea, the Mississippi, the largest river in North America, flows across a huge flood plain. Forests of water-loving trees have grown up in the waters of lakes and channels cut off from the main route of the river. The local name for these damp, swampy areas is bayous.

△ The plain of Lombardy in northern Italy is the flood plain of
the Po River. Villages and farms are often flooded, as in this
picture taken in 1987.

In many parts of the world, the river is very important to the people who live beside it. In the desert country of Egypt, the Nile River provides water for drinking and for irrigating the land for growing plants. In the tropical forests of Brazil and Zaïre, a journey by boat was once the only way to travel inland from the sea.

Many big cities in Europe and North America grew up along the banks of rivers. Ships and barges use the rivers to bring goods to and from the cities.

▷Most of Egypt is desert, except for a strip of land along the Nile River. The people who farm here depend on the floods each year to bring water and fertile silt down river.

The farmers use bucket-wheels and pumps to lift the water from the river. They have built canals and ditches to spread water from the Nile into the farmlands.

△ Factories use river water for making products such as paints. But they also pour waste liquids into rivers to be carried away to the ocean. Some of these liquids contain harmful chemicals which make the river water poisonous to plants and animals. They dirty, or pollute, the rivers.

Toward the ocean

At last the river reaches the coast after bending and winding its way across the flood plain. The clear fresh water that gathered in the mountains far away mixes with the salt water of the ocean. The river bed meets the seashore and forms a wide sandy area of calm water known as an estuary.

◁The river reaches the sea in an opening called a mouth, like this one at Ballyness Bay in Ireland. If the rivermouth is very wide, it forms a broad area of water known as an estuary. As the ocean tide goes out and comes in, the estuary is filled with fresh water at low tide and with salt water at high tide.

▷Many kinds of plants and animals live around estuaries. The plants have to be able to survive in both fresh and salt water.

Here, at the estuary of the Rhône River in France, millions of migrating birds from northern Europe stop to feed on water plants and animals. They then continue their journey to Africa.

Where the river meets the ocean, sand and silt is washed from the land. Sometimes the mouth of the river is blocked by sandbanks. The river has to cut channels through them to reach the ocean. The result is an area of wet, marshy land and river channels called a delta.

Although the river has reached the end of its journey, the story doesn't end here. The water from the river flows into the ocean. And from the surface of the ocean, water is drawn up into the air. It is carried back over the land and falls as rain, keeping the river flowing.

▷ Probably the most famous delta in the world is that of the Nile River. From high above the Earth, the delta appears as a broad triangular mass between the yellow desert sand and the blue Mediterranean Sea. The triangle shape is like the Greek letter delta, hence the name of this river feature.

◁ At the seashore, ocean currents wash sand along the beach. When this moving sand reaches a river mouth it may collect across the mouth in a long thin sandbank or spit. The river current keeps the river mouth from being completely clogged with beach sand.

Glossary

Bayou A sluggish stretch of water cut off from the main part of a river or lake.

Cascade A series of waterfalls one after the other and close together.

Current A movement of water in a particular direction. The flow of a river produces many currents. Some travel along the length of the river, others across it.

Dam A wall built across a river or a stream to hold back the water. A dam can be built to control the amount of water flowing in the river and so prevent flooding. It can also be used to direct the flow of water towards waterwheels or turbines and so provide power.

Delta An area of sandbanks and islands of gravel that sometimes occurs at the mouth of a river.

Dynamo A machine for making electricity. It usually consists of two magnets, one of which spins round inside the other. The two magnetic fields working against each other produce an electric current. A *turbine* makes the first magnet spin round.

Estuary The broad mouth of a river that can be full of fresh water when the tide is out but full of salt water when the tide has come in.

Flood When a river becomes too full, it floods. Water bursts over the banks on to the surrounding countryside.

Flood plain A broad flat area of land that is covered with silt and sand brought down by a river and dropped when the river is in flood.

Glacier A mass of ice that forms when snow is packed down hard in a hollow on a mountainside. A glacier moves downhill under its own weight, like a river of ice.

Irrigation Watering dry land to allow crops to grow.

Meander A wide loop or bend in a slowly flowing river.

Mouth The place where a river enters the ocean.

Oxbow A crescent or horseshoe-shaped lake on a river flood plain.

Rapid A stretch of very rough and fast-flowing water in a river.

Silt Fine grains of sand and soil that are washed down by a river.

Source The place where a river begins.

Spit A tongue-like bank of sand built up by ocean currents across the mouth of a river.

Spring A place where rock is completely and permanently soaked with water so that when rain falls, water bubbles up from the ground and flows as a tiny stream. A spring can also form at the tip of a glacier as the ice melts.

Turbine A machine that is turned by the movement of water.

Valley The channel or groove in which a river flows. High up in mountains, river valleys are often narrow and steep-sided. On low land, valleys are usually wide and have low, gently sloping sides.

Waterfall A falling curtain of water where a river or stream drops down a cliff.

Facts about rivers

Longest river The two longest rivers in the world are the Amazon in South America and the Nile in north Africa. Both are more than 6,435 km (4,000 miles) long. It is difficult to measure which is the longest because no one is sure where the sources and main river channels are.

Longest estuary The world's longest estuary is that of the Ob River in the USSR. It is 885 km (550 miles) long and 80 km (50 miles) wide.

Largest delta In Bangladesh and West Bengal, India, the Ganges and Brahmaputra rivers meet at the coast to form the world's largest delta. It covers an area some 480 km (300 miles) long and 160 km (100 miles) wide.

Highest waterfall The Salto Angel Falls in Venezuela, with a drop of almost 1,000 m (3,300 ft), is the world's highest waterfall.

Deepest gorge The deepest gorge in the world is El Cañón de Colca in Peru, it is more than 2½ miles deep.

Biggest dam The 30 m (98 ft) high New Cornelia Dam in Arizona, required the most earth and rubble to build, but the largest concrete dam in the world is the Grand Coulee Dam in the state of Washington. This is 167 m (550 ft) high and measures 1,272 m (4,173 ft) in length along the top of the dam.

Worst flood The world's worst flood was in 1877 when the Hwang-ho River in China burst its banks and killed 900,000 people.

▷The view from an aircraft flying above the Amazon River in Brazil. Here the river has formed two large bends or meanders so that it flows in an S-shape. A lake is forming on one of the meanders as the river tries to cut its way forward.

Index

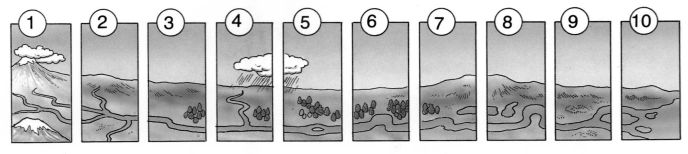

PRINTED IN BELGIUM BY
proost
INTERNATIONAL BOOK PRODUCTION

910
B   Bender, Lionel
         River

$11.90

3

910
B   Bender, Lionel
         River

$11.90

DATE	BORROWER'S NAME	
1-28-92	Quang Le	T-7
	Brian	